CURIOSITII
LONDON AND
WESTMINSTER

A GUIDE TO THE UNUSUAL

CHARLES BIRD

First published in 2003 by S B Publications
19 Grove Road, Seaford, East Sussex BN25 1TP
telephone: 01323 893498
fax: 01323 893860
email: sbpublications@tiscali.co.uk

ISBN 1-85770-237-9

Typeset by JEM Editorial, JEMedit@AOL.com

Printed by Pageturn Ltd, East Sussex, BN3 7EG. Tel: (01273) 821500

CONTENTS

City of London

City of Westminster

Photographs
> *front cover*:   Duke of Wellington's Statue at Cornhill
>   Statue of Queen Victoria, Queen's Gardens
> *back cover*:   Little Ben, Victoria Street
> *title page*:   The Wood Street Comptor, see page 34

PREFACE

Throughout the twin cities of London and Westminster there are innumerable items of interest to the Londoner and visitor alike. Many are passed every day without a second, or even a first glance. These are the forgotten, missed or unknown facets of these two great cities. In this book I have endeavoured to seek them out and to draw the reader's attention to them. While this book was not devised as a book of walks, the contents page suggests an order in which several places, within easy walking distance to each other, may be visited.

1 – City Dragons, Victoria Embankment

This dragon, and its twin on the opposite side of the roadway, were cast in 1848 for the Coal Exchange in Lower Thames Street. When the building was unmercifully demolished in 1962 they were saved and, in the following year, erected on the Victoria Embankment on stone plinths to mark the boundary of the City of London. The inscription on the plinth reads:

> *These dragons represent a constituent part of the armorial bearings of the City of London and have been erected here to indicate the western boundary of the City. This commemorative plaque was unveiled by the Rt. Hon. The Lord Mayor Sir Ralph Edgar Perring on 16th October 1963. The dragons were formerly mounted above the entrance of the Coal Exchange.*

The idea of having the dragons as markers was so popularly received by the public that a cast was made from which aluminium markers were made and placed around the City's boundaries. They may now be seen at Holborn Bar, Farringdon Street at the junction with Farringdon Road, Moorgate, Bishopsgate, Aldgate High Street and at the Southwark end of London Bridge.

Dragons made their first appearance in the City as supporters to the Corporation's bearings in 1609. The Arms of the City of London are not strictly legal. No Grant of Arms was ever made to the City. The shield existed 100 years before the incorporation of the College of Arms, but its use has since been recognised. However, the crest, the motto and the dragon supporters were all added at a much later date and have no authority whatsoever.

2 – WEATHERVANE, QUEEN VICTORIA STREET

The former parish church of St Nicholas is now occupied by the Cole Abbey Presbyterian Church of Scotland, and is known as the Wee Freebies. A reminder that St Nicholas is the patron saint of sailors can be seen on the roof of the building where a weathervane depicts a grain-bearing ship. In the hold of the model is a bushel of grain. Previously, the weathervane was on the church of St Michael Queenhithe, but after demolition of that church in 1867 it was installed here at the church of St Nicholas Cole Abbey.

3 – QUEENHITHE DOCK

An inlet of the Thames, Queenhithe is one of the oldest docks of the City of London. It was founded in the time of King Alfred, *c*848-901, who named it Ethelredhythe after his son-in-law, the Alderman of Mercia. King Stephen gave the hithe to William of Ypres who in turn bestowed it to the Convent of the Holy Trinity, Aldgate. Henry III compelled the ships of the Cinque Ports (south coast ports which were granted privileges in return for supplying the king with a navy) to bring all their corn to the hithe. It was then named Queen's Hithe, and the receipts formed part of the Queen's 'pocket money'.

The dock served the City well until such times as the large ships were no longer able to negotiate their way through London Bridge. Then, the Upper Pool, the river up to London Bridge, became the main docking and unloading centre of commerce.

From the dockside the view across the river reveals the new Globe Theatre, and the Tate Modern art gallery which opened in 2000 in the old Bankside power station. Bankside, operational from 1963 to 1980, was designed by Sir Giles Gilbert Scott. The gallery is linked to the City by the Millennium Foot Bridge, inaugurated by the Queen in May 2000.

4 – TRUST MARK AT LONDON BRIDGE

Early bridges were built by generous benefactors and maintained by the collection of pontage tax (bridge tax), the levy being based on the number of people and animals using the bridge. Peter of Colechurch, priest of St Mary Colechurch in the City's Poultry, and chaplain to the Chapel of Corpus Christi, initiated the building of London's first stone bridge in 1176. From its completion in 1209 until late in the sixteenth century the bridge fund received a multitude of gifts and bequests in money and in properties from the pious people of the City. It was thought that to endow such projects as bridges and chapels would help one's life in the next world.

A trust was set up to benefit the City's four bridges – Southwark, Blackfriars, Tower and London – and lessen the tax burden on the inhabitants and the commercial premises of the City. The trust's mark may be seen inscribed in the stone of the Bridge House at London Bridge on the north side of the river.

NEAR THIS SITE STOOD THE SHOP
BELONGING TO THOMAS FARYNER.
THE KING'S BAKER. IN WHICH THE
GREAT FIRE OF SEPTEMBER 1666 BEGAN.

PRESENTED BY
THE WORSHIPFUL COMPANY OF BAKERS
TO MARK THE 500th ANNIVERSARY OF
THEIR CHARTER GRANTED BY
KING HENRY VII IN 1486

5 – Bakers' Company plaque at Pudding Lane

On the corner of Monument Street and Pudding Lane the
Worshipful Company of Bakers erected a plaque on the side of
Faryner House to commemorate the 500th anniversary of its charter
in 1486. The plaque records that 'Near this site stood the shop
belonging to Thomas Faryner the King's baker in which the Great
Fire of London of September 1666 began'.

The fire spread from the shop to a nearby inn where hay was being
stored for the horses and for bed palliasses. With a strong wind
blowing from the east, and the lack of any efficient fire fighting
equipment, the fire devastated the City, five-sixths of which was
burnt to the ground in three days. The fire was no respecter of
church, livery hall, or commercial building, and it was left to
architect Christopher Wren to help rebuild London.

6 – St Dunstan's Church Garden, St Dunstan's Hill

The original church of St Dunstan in the East was built not later than the thirteenth century, possibly earlier, although Hennessy's *Novum Repertorium* records the first rector as John de Pretelweille (Prittlewell, Essex), who vacated the living in 1310. The medieval church was one of the Peculiars of the City owing allegiance to the Archbishop of Canterbury and not the Bishop of London.

The church was destroyed in the Great Fire of 1666 and rebuilt by Wren, and again in 1817 when the walls of the nave showed signs of collapsing. It was bombed in the Second World War and not rebuilt, but the ruins were transformed into a garden of peace and rest.

On the south outside wall there is a plaque recording the planting of a fig tree in 1937. It is the only commemoration of George VI's Coronation left in the City.

7 – STATUE OF EMPEROR TRAJAN, TRINITY SQUARE, TOWER HILL

The late Reverend Philip (Tubby) Clayton, rector of All Hallows-by-the-Tower, founder of the Toc H movement, found this eighteenth century replica sculpture of the Emperor Trajan in a Southampton junk yard. He gave it to the Tower Hill Improvement Trust and it was erected here in 1980. The figure is bare-headed and wears the short tunic of a Roman general with a short sword under the left arm. The head is Trajan's but the body is that of Augustus.

8 – SITE OF THE SCAFFOLD ON TOWER HILL

This place has been described as one of the bloodiest sites of all London. For celebrity executions, stands were erected for spectators to watch, jeer or cheer the condemned as they walked up Tower Hill. Sometimes the stands were so overcrowded that they collapsed from the sheer weight of the watchers, and on more than one occasion a beheading was delayed while the stand was repaired.

Around the inside perimeter is a Roll of Dishonour, listing the most famous or infamous names of those executed. Simon of Sudbury, Archbishop of Canterbury 1375-1381, and Sir Robert Hales, Grand Prior of the Order of St John of Jerusalem, are the first two listed. Without trial or jury, they were summarily executed on the orders

of Wat Tyler, the insurrectionist, during the rebellion against the Poll Tax of 1381. But they were not the first to be executed here. Earlier, Simon Burley, tutor to Richard II, was beheaded for treason. The last person executed at Tower Hill was Simon Fraser, Lord Lovat, in 1747. He failed in his support of Bonnie Prince Charlie in the uprising of 1745. His was also the last public beheading in England.

The scaffold was later replaced by a gallows which claimed its last victims during the 'No Popery' riots of the 1780s. The last felons hanged were a one-armed soldier and two prostitutes who were found guilty of taking part in a drunken attack on a Roman Catholic inn-keeper on Tower Hill.

Around the site are pleasant public gardens that are popular with city workers enjoying summer lunch breaks. Within the bounds of the gardens are two war memorials – one a Mercantile Marine memorial, designed by Edwin Lutyens, for the merchant seamen who died in the First World War, and the other, designed by Edward Maufe, for seamen killed in the Second World War.

9 – War Department boundary mark, Muscovy Street

Outside the City Wall there were a number of 'liberties' – places where people could live, work and play without being under the jurisdiction of the City authorities. Some were part of the precincts of monastic establishments, others were of a more personal and private nature. One of these was the Liberty of the Fleet (Prison) where ex-prisoners and their families were allowed to live. Another was, and still is, the Liberty of the Tower of London where the governor, acting on behalf of the monarch, is the authority. Each of the liberties areas was clearly marked at its boundaries with metal plaques.

The number nine mark is the Tower of London boundary mark. Every three years the Tower's chaplain and choir, accompanied by an escort of Yeoman Warders and members of the public, beat the bounds. This is an ancient ceremony in which each of the marks is visited to see that it is still in good condition and to remind 'all and sundry' where the boundaries are. This was, and still is, an important factor for those wishing to use the church or chapel for weddings, baptisms and funerals.

10 – BUST OF SAMUEL PEPYS, SEETHING LANE

Samuel Pepys was born on February 23, 1633, in Salisbury Court, off Fleet Street, the fifth and first surviving son of a London tailor, and

he was baptised in the parish church of St Bride, Fleet Street. Pepys was educated at St Paul's School and Magdalene College, Cambridge, after which he entered into service in the Navy Office. He wrote his famous Diary between January 1660 and May 1669.

The diarist was a founder member of the Royal Society, Master of the Worshipful Company of Clothworkers and an Elder Brother of the Most Glorious and Undivided Trinity (Trinity House). He left his library to Magdalene College, and it is here that his Diary, first deciphered and edited in 1825, can still be seen.

The bust in Seething Lane Garden is the work of the Swedish sculptor Karin Jonzen, and was erected by the Samuel Pepys Club and public subscriptions in 1983. Before the Annual Commemoration Service in St Olave's church in May, the president or chairman of the club lays a wreath at the foot of the bust. During the service the Lord Mayor of London places a wreath under the memorial to Pepys in the church.

11 – Skull and crossbones, St Olave, Hart Street

An archway entrance to the churchyard from Seething Lane leads to the south doorway of the church. The arch is inscribed in memory of those members of the parish who died of a plague in 1658. The skulls and crossbones above the archway inspired Charles Dickens to re-name the church 'St Ghastly Grim' in *The Uncommercial Traveller*.

To the right of the gateway the noticeboard records that on September 14, 1658, Mother Goose was buried in the church. The records show nothing more about her, except that she died of the plague.

Samuel Pepys lived, with his wife, in the Navy Office situated in the lane across the road from the church, and referred to St Olave's as 'our own church'.

12 – NAVY OFFICE PEW, ST OLAVE, HART STREET

On the south external wall of the church, sandwiched between two windows, can be seen a blocked-up entrance to the gallery of the church. This was the entrance to the Navy Office pew. The inscription reads: 'Entrance to the South Gallery and the Navy Office Pew often mentioned in the Diary of Samuel Pepys.' The Diary reads:

> *11th November 1660:*
> *'(Lord's day) To church into our new gallery, the first time it was used. There being no woman this day, we sat in the foremost pew behind our servants, and I hope it will not always be so, it not handsome for our servants to sit equal with us.'*
> *23rd December 1660:*
> *'(Lord's day) In the morning to church, where our pew all covered with rosemary and bays. A stranger made a dull sermon.'*

13 – ALDGATE PUMP AT LEADENHALL STREET

The pump is at the junction of Fenchurch Street and Leadenhall Street, near the site of St Michael's, Aldgate, a church that has long since disappeared. In medieval times a holy well was attached to the church. This was fed from the same source as the pump. Early in the twentieth century the original pump and well were removed after the water was tested following complaints of its strange taste. It was discovered that part of the water's underground journey from the 'northern hills of London' – Hampstead – passed through several burial grounds. Bones had fallen into the water, giving it that extra calcium taste! The present-day pump, 6ft from the site of the original pump, is supplied with water from Thames Water's reservoirs. The head of the wolf on the water spout is said to be in memory of the last wolf shot in the City of London.

14 – St Edmund's church spire, Lombard Street

History does not tell us when exactly St Edmund's was founded or why its dedication was chosen. Supposedly it was called St Edmund's after the body of Edmund, King of East Anglia, was brought here for fear that the marauders who shot him to death with arrows might return and steal the body. If this story is true then

there was a church here in the late ninth century.

After the Great Fire of 1666 the neighbouring church of St Nicholas Acons was not rebuilt, and the parish was added to St Edmund's. Wren's rebuilding of St Edmund's following the fire included a spire in the shape of a medieval lighthouse, in honour of St Nicholas, patron saint of lighthouse keepers.

15 – LOMBARD STREET'S HANGING SIGNS

Lombard (Lumbard) Street, became the home of the men of Lombardy, Italy, who in the early Middle Ages established a wool market here in the City of London. Merchant bankers were also prominent members of the community. At the expulsion of the Jews during the reign of Edward I the Lombardians became the main

money-lenders and bankers of London. Their sign, depicting three balls, has been the symbol of pawnbrokers ever since.

The street has been described as the finest in Elizabethan London. Historian Thomas Carlyle called it 'the street of the greatest credit in England'. John Heywood's *Edward IV*, published in 1600, refers to the signs of the street:

> *Here's Lombard Street, and here's the Pelican;*
> *And here's the Phoenix in the Pelican's nest.*

Signs still seen today include: 'A Cat and a Fiddle', a reference to the thirteenth century knight, Caton le Fidele, of the time of Edward I, who was a faithful (fidele) servant of the King; and 'TSB 1810' on the premises where the Trustee Savings Bank was founded.

The most prominent survivor is the grasshopper on number 68; buildings on this site

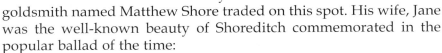

have been used for banking for more than 450 years. Sir Thomas Gresham set up a goldsmith's business 'at the sign of the grasshopper' in 1549, the sign being adopted from the crest of the Gresham Family. Tradition tells that in 1461 a goldsmith named Matthew Shore traded on this spot. His wife, Jane was the well-known beauty of Shoreditch commemorated in the popular ballad of the time:

> *In Lombard Street I once did dwell,*
> *Where many gallants did behold,*

As London yet can witness well,
My beauty in a shop of gold.

Number 71, the Lloyds Bank building, has the familiar black horse sign outside. Originally this was the house sign of Humphrey Stokes, a goldsmith who set up his business at number 53 in the seventeenth century. He is identified in the first *London Directory* as 'Stocks', as a keeper of running cashes. Samuel Pepys records:

I out to Lombard Street and there received £2,200 and brought it home, and contrary to expectation received £35 for the use of £2,000 for the quarter of the year . . . to the care and security at my home, and demandable at two days warning . . .

John Bland succeeded Stokes and later transferred the business to his son, who traded under the name of Bland and Barnett. Over succeeding years they, and other financial businesses, merged, finally ending up as Lloyds, which took over the sign of Humphrey Stokes – the black horse at number 71. Thus the sign of the little goldsmith of Lombard Street is now the emblem of one of the greatest banking houses in the world.

The anchor at number 78 is the Christian sign for hope; it was often

adopted as a part of the sign for Hope and Anchor taverns. On this site in the eighteenth century were the offices of bankers Willis, Percival and Company, who let the upper rooms to the Society for the Relief of Poor Pious Clergy. Both establishments have now passed on.

16 – GARRAWAY'S COFFEE SHOP SIGN, EXCHANGE ALLEY

Thomas Garraway set up auction rooms here in 1669. Many of the goods came from the Hudson's Bay Company. Ships, and their contents too, were offered for sale, as well as salvaged goods. At this house, in 1651, tea was first sold in England, the proprietor announcing that to drink it was a sure cure for all ills! In the 1670s tea cost £10 a pound. In the nineteenth century the merchants here were drug brokers, Turkish merchants and ship brokers who used it as their London address.

17 – Duke of Wellington's statue at Cornhill

There are several memorials to and statues of the Iron Duke in and around London. None is finer than the equestrian statue by Sir Francis Chantry at the foot of Cornhill, outside the Royal Exchange building.

Standing on a high pedestal of Peterhead granite, it was erected by the Corporation of London – not in recognition of his victories on the battlefield, but for the duke's help in getting an Act through Parliament for the rebuilding of London Bridge.

It should be compared with the sculptor's George IV in Trafalgar Square, and not without good reason. Both statues are identical (except for the heads), with the figures dressed in nothing of a very definite description from which to show their rank or position. Each wears a short coat and cloak, no shoes or boots or stirrups, no

saddle – only a cloth – and a single rein. Both statues were finished after Chantry's death in 1841, by which time he had completed only a quarter-sized model of the Wellington statue, a full-sized head and the horse. Henry Weekes finished the commission, doubtless using other casts in Chantry's studio in Eccleston Square, Victoria. The duke's statue cost £10,000, which may seem excessive considering the bronze came from French guns captured by Wellington and given by the government.

18 – THE LONDON STONE, CANNON STREET

Experts have, over the years, agreed to disagree about the stone's origin. Theories range from it being a Druid's altar stone to a Roman milestone from the Forum of Londinium. Whatever the answer, English Heritage has it listed as a Grade II monument in the care and upkeep of the current owner of the building (the OCBC – Overseas Chinese Banking Corporation). Shakespeare makes a passing reference to the stone in Henry VI, Part 2 when the stage direction reads:

> *Enter Iacke (sic) Cade, and strikes his staffe on London Stone.*

Jack Cade was the leader of a Kentish revolt against corrupt courts, government maladministration, and heavy taxation. He led a party of men from Ashford, Kent, to London and, having changed his name to Mortimer, took the City by storm, only to leave after an amnesty was granted to the rebels. Cade was hunted down, killed and buried anonymously in unconsecrated soil.

According to the plaque on the street side, the stone was moved from where Cannon Street Station now stands in 1742, to the wall of St Swithun's church opposite. When the church was demolished in 1962 and the present building erected in its place, the stone was enclosed in the wall.

19 – Boy with a goose, Poultry

Poultry was the extension of the Cheapside market of the Middle Ages where chickens, geese and other fowls were sold. The Boy with the Goose, by Sir William Dick Reid, stands proudly on the head office of the former Midland Bank (now HSBC) designed by Sir Edwin Lutyens in 1924, and completed just before the outbreak of the Second World War in 1939.

20 – PAUL'S CROSS , ST PAUL'S CATHEDRAL

'Here stood Paul's Cross' reads the inscription in the north-east corner of the cathedral's churchyard. Once there was a simple cross at the entrance to the churchyard in order to remind citizens passing by to pray for the repose of the souls of the departed. Stow, in his *Survay* of 1598, wrote that here in 1259 Henry III ordered that the mayor should summon all boys over the age of twelve to swear an allegiance to the King 'at Paul's Cross hard by the cathedral'.

Learned sermons and other theological discourses were read from the cross and, in 1617, the Lady Markham was made to stand at the cross for three days, clothed only in a white sheet. Her crime? She had married one of her servants – but her husband was alive at the time. Until its destruction in 1643, by fanatic Puritans who deemed it idolatrous, the cross was used as an open-air pulpit – described by Thomas Carlyle as being 'The Times' of the Middle Ages.

21 – CLOISTERS FOUNDATIONS, ST PAUL'S CATHEDRAL

Outlined in the grass on the south side of St Paul's are the foundations of the cloisters from the time when the Order of Secular Canons staffed the cathedral. An unusual feature was the placing of the Chapter House in the centre of the cloister garth. The cloisters were seriously damaged in the Great Fire of 1666, having fallen into disrepair after the Dissolution of the Monasteries in the sixteenth century.

22 – STATUE OF ST THOMAS BECKET, ST PAUL'S CATHEDRAL

Becket, 'London's own saint', became the fortieth Archbishop of Canterbury in 1161, but was never Bishop of London. He was born in Cheapside of wealthy Norman parents, educated at Merton Abbey, Surrey, and rose to the office of Chancellor and finally to Archbishop. His quarrels with Henry II led eventually to his murder in Canterbury Cathedral by the King's order. Edward Bainbridge Copal's recumbent figure (of 1973) shows Becket falling to the ground. 'Who will rid me of this turbulent priest?' Henry is supposed to have uttered. More likely the words were composed by TS Eliot for his dramatic play, *Murder in the Cathedral*.

23 – STATUE OF QUEEN ANNE, ST PAUL'S CATHEDRAL

The much admired and maligned statue of Queen Anne stands outside the west front of the cathedral and has the queen looking down Ludgate Hill towards Fleet Street. The original figure by Francis Bird was erected here in 1712, but was replaced by the present 'exact replica' by Richard Belt in 1886 – the first having become dilapidated. The Belt statue was paid for by Augustus Hare, a writer of guides to London and Rome; in return he claimed Bird's statue and removed it to Holmhurst, St Leonard's.

The figures around the base of the statue represent England, France, Ireland and North America as, at that time, Anne still regarded herself as queen of all four countries.

24 – Panyer Boy stone, Paternoster Steps

Here a young naked boy is depicted sitting astride his panyer basket on a stone that was erected here, or nearby, in 1688. The occupation of panyer boys was to sell and deliver bread. In the fourteenth century a proclamation was made against the sale of bread in the houses of bakers; it could be sold only in the 'king's markets'. However, bread was also sold on the streets in baskets or panyers, and this was just the job for young boys who could, and did, move swiftly through the narrow and often crowded streets and lanes of the City.

The inscription on the stone reads:

> *When ye have sought*
> *The Citty Round*
> *Yet still ths is*
> *The Highest Ground*
> *August the 27*
> *1688*

In fact, the highest point of the City is at the top of Cornhill where it meets Gracechurch, Leadenhall and Bishopsgate Streets – but only by 1ft.

25 – GUY OF WARWICK'S STONE, WARWICK LANE

On the corner of Newgate Street and Warwick Lane stood the London palace of the Earls of Warwick, and here can be seen a stone plaque of 1668 depicting a Grand Old Man of earlier days – Guy of Warwick, who died in 1315. He was one of the seven earls who attached their seals to a protest to the Pope rejecting papal authority in Scottish political affairs. He was also responsible for the banishment of Piers Gaveston, the intimate friend of Edward II. Guy's famous descendant, Richard Neville, Earl of Warwick, was instrumental in placing Edward IV on the throne in 1461 and in restoring Henry VI in 1470. He was killed in the Battle of Barnet in 1471.

26 – MARCONI MEMORIAL PLAQUE, NEWGATE STREET

Guglielmo Marconi, discouraged by the Italian government's apathy towards his invention of 'wire-less telegraphy', arrived in London to seek his fortune in 1896. Within a few weeks of his arrival the young man was invited by the General Post Office to demonstrate his invention. This he did from the roof of a previous building on this site, to a receiver half a mile away, on July 27. Within seconds the message was relayed back again. The GPO men were deeply impressed by what they saw. Marconi returned to his house in Hereford Road, W2 where he completed the patent for the world's first application for wireless telegraphy.

The plaque is on the new building at the corner where the lane meets the street.

27 – WEATHERVANE, ST MARY LE BOW, CHEAPSIDE

The fine dragon weathervane on St Mary le Bow's steeple is easily visible from many quarters of the City. The vane is 8ft 10in long, made of copper gilt and has a red and white Greek cross painted on the underside of its wings.

According to an old tradition in the City should the dragon meet the grasshopper (on the Royal Exchange) a national disaster will occur. The last recorded time that they met was when both the vane, and the grasshopper sign, were taken to a builder's yard to be cleaned. The nation was not overtaken by disaster on that occasion.

In a pamphlet of the day, *Ecclesia et facto, or a dialogue between the Dragon of Bow Church and the Grasshopper of the Exchange* (1698), the dragon represented the High Church of England, and the grasshopper the dissenters. The opening words are:

Tell me, proud insect, since thou canst fly,
By what assistance thou art hopped so high

28 – Bee keystone, Honey Lane, Cheapside

Medieval Cheapside was the main shopping centre for the City of London. It was lined with shops from end to end, with stalls outside and side streets that catered for 'specialised shopping'. Such a side turning was Honey Lane, where the excess product of the bees of the Wax Chandlers Company was sold as a sweetener to housewives who were not rich enough to pay the price of imported sugar. After the Great Fire in 1666, a new market in Honey Lane replaced much of Cheapside Market, both to relieve traffic congestion and to appease inhabitants who considered the market to be a 'great annoyance'.

The keystone to the (modern) archway that leads to a truncated Honey Lane today shows a busy bee collecting its honey.

29 – THE WOOD STREET COMPTOR

Opposite Goldsmith Street in Wood Street there is an archway leading to a courtyard, Mitre Court, where once stood a comptor. Comptors were prisons under the personal supervision of the sheriffs, and were used to incarcerate debtors' rather than criminals. Where, in the building, debtors were held, depended on their financial status. Those with some money, able to pay their way while inside, were allotted rooms above ground, but the insolvent were confined below ground (in the dungeons) until they could pay their way out.

The canopy and stairs in the courtyard lead down to some of the remaining cells. Today, the underground space is used to store wine, and occasionally it is possible for sightseers to visit if they are lucky to be there when the comptor is open.

30 – WAX CHANDLERS' HALL, GRESHAM STREET

The Worshipful Company of Wax Chandlers, founded in 1358, was the supplier of pure beeswax candles to the cathedral and churches of the Cities of London and Westminster, to the houses of rich merchants and to the livery halls.

Above the entrance to Wax Chandlers' Hall (built in 1958) can be seen the company's armorial bearings of three mortars royal with spikes in which to fix candles, and the motto 'Truth is the light'. At the bottom of the flagstaff is a plaque showing a hive and the bees returning after their days' work is done.

31 – Sir Ebenezer Howard plaque, London Wall, Moorgate

Ebenezer Howard was the originator of the garden-city movement and founder of Letchworth (1903) and Welwyn (1919) garden cities. Appalled by the overcrowding of cities and their unhealthy conditions, Howard founded the Garden City Movement in 1899 to promote his ideal of both residential and industrial development being surrounded by a rural belt.

The plaque says that near the spot on London Wall, at 62 Fore Street, Howard was born on January 29, 1850.

<u>32 – SITE OF ST OLAVE'S, SILVER STREET (NOBLE STREET)</u>

Both street and church have disappeared, the former in post Second
World War developments and the latter in the Great Fire of London,
1666. Silver Street is now the upper end of Noble Street and the
church site is on the corner at the junction of Noble Street and
London Wall. An open space marks the site where there is an
inscribed stone on which is written, beneath a skull and two
crossbones:

> *THIS WAS THE PARISH CHURCH OF ST OLAVE SILVER STREET*
> *DESTROYED BY THE DREADFULL FIRE IN THE YEAR 1666*

33 – FOUNDATIONS AT ST MARY ALDERMANBURY

The church was founded in the twelfth century and has a long time connection with the Aldermen of the City of London whose 'bury' (house) was, and still is within the parish boundary. Their rebuilt 'house', lovingly known as the Brandy Glass, can be seen in Guildhall Yard. The medieval church was burnt down in the Great Fire and rebuilt by Wren. This church suffered badly in December 1940 and was eventually demolished and shipped to the United States of America. It was re-erected as the Chapel for Westminster College, University of Fulton, Missouri, where it stands as a memorial to Sir Winston Churchill. (It was here that he made his famous 'Iron Curtain' speech 5 March 1946). The foundations of the church have now been laid out as a garden.

34 – HEMINGE AND CONDELL MEMORIAL, ALDERMANBURY

Buried either in the church or the churchyard lie Heminge and Condell, whose contribution to English literature was to print the original folio editions of Shakespeare's comedies, histories and tragedies from 1623. This monument, which is in the former churchyard of St Mary Aldermanbury, on the corner of Love Lane and Aldermanbury, is topped with a bust of Shakespeare by Charles J Allen (1895).

John Heminge, the first to play Falstaff in *Henry IV,* and Henry Condell were fellow actors and friends of Shakespeare. Heminge was also part of the syndicate that bought The Theatre in Shoreditch and re-erected it in Southwark as The Globe. With the two Burbages and Shakespeare, he had a house built alongside the theatre. Their names collectively or singly appeared on tenancy leases for the first two decades of the seventeenth century.

35 – TOWER OF ST ALBAN'S CHURCH, WOOD STREET

The parish dates back to Saxon times and the church may originally have been the chapel for the nearby palace of King Athelstan (Adelstan) in the tenth century. Inigo Jones, the Palladian architect, rebuilt the church in the early seventeenth century, but it was destroyed in the Great Fire of 1666. Wren then rebuilt the church in the Gothic style; in 1867 Sir Gilbert Scott added an apse and completely re-fitted the interior. The church was reduced to a shell in the blitz of 1940; it was demolished and only the tower remains.

Today the tower stands alone on a road island, opposite the Wood Street Police Station. It has been adapted internally to provide residential and office space.

36 – ROMAN CITY WALL, (SILVER STREET) NOBLE STREET

In 61AD Boadicea, Queen of the Iceni tribe, razed the (unfortified) City to the ground in revenge for the despoiling of her daughters by the Roman overlords of the time. Sixty years later the Romans built the first complete stone wall around the City.

Part of the wall of the City and part of the wall that pre-dated it may be seen here in Noble Street. The earlier wall enclosed an area of the Cripplegate Fort that was built to house the occupying Roman soldiers. These remains came to light during archaeological excavations in the late 1940s, together with two distinct layers of wood ash – from Boadicea's visit and from the Great Fire of 1666.

37 – WELLINGTON ARCH, HYDE PARK CORNER

This arch, at the end of Constitution Hill, was designed by Decimus Burton and erected here in 1828 as a memorial to the Iron Duke – Arthur Wellesley (1769-1852), first Duke of Wellington, victor of the Battle of Waterloo. An equestrian statue of the duke riding his favourite horse, Copenhagen, was placed on the top of the arch. This was later removed to an army parade ground in Aldershot, where it still stands today. A bronze group, The Quadriga, by Adrian Jones (a former officer in the 3rd Hussars), stands in its place.

A roof terrace has been added from which there are views over Hyde Park, Green Park and St James's Park as well as much of the surrounding area.

38 – ROYAL ARTILLERY MEMORIAL, HYDE PARK CORNER

The Royal Artillery memorial on the road island at Hyde Park Corner is surmounted by a stone field gun pointing skywards at such an angle that ,should it be capable of firing, its shell would land in the heart of the Somme where thousands of gunners died in the trenches of the First World War.

The memorial was designed by Charles Sargeant Jagger, assisted by Lionel Pearson, and carved from a great block of Portland stone. At its base lies a dead soldier, his body covered by a cloak, and around the base are statues of a young officer, a cloaked driver and an ammunition carrier.

39-40 – ROYAL ARTILLERY MEMORIAL, HYDE PARK CORNER

The memorial is full of pleasant surprises and time spent wandering around it will reveal small items of interest. One of these is the figure of the Blessed Virgin Mary with the Christ Child on her lap at the Hyde Park end of the base of the memorial.

A little way from this is, carved in the stone, a mess-tin, knife, fork and spoon stuck in a sandbag above which is an army rum-jar with the letters SRD. An old soldier once said that the letters stood for 'Seldom Reaches Destination'; actually they meant 'Supply Reserve Depot'. I prefer the old soldier's version.

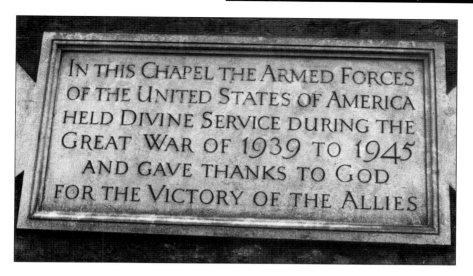

41 – GROSVENOR CHAPEL PLAQUE, SOUTH AUDLEY STREET

The chapel is one of a small number of proprietary chapels left in London. It was built in 1730 by Benjamin Timbrell as part of the scheme for Grosvenor Square. Such chapels were built away from parish churches, and operated on a licence from the bishop. Their independence was maintained by the renting of pews to the congregation.

The inscription on the exterior west wall records the use of the chapel during the Second World War by the USA armed forces.

42 – I am the Only Running Footman pub, Charles Street

This very rare if not unique name for a public house calls to mind a strange and strenuous occupation by a servant in days gone by. To facilitate the speedy, safe journey of his master, a running footman would run ahead of the nobleman's coach to pay the tolls, thereby allowing the journey to continue uninterrupted, and to be ready on arrival to assist the passengers to alight. If the journey were by night, the running footman carried a flaming torch in order to ensure the way ahead was clear of highwaymen and vagrants. He was capable of running in excess of six miles an hour on good terrain, and was helped on his way by a drink of wine and egg-white that he carried in the end of his wand. The position flourished in the seventeenth century and was last used by the fourth Lord of Queensbury up to his death in 1810.

43 – BURLINGTON ARCADE, PICCADILLY

Samuel Ware, architect to the Dukes of Devonshire, designed and built the arcade at the request of Lord George Cavendish – to stop members of the public, it was said, from throwing their rubbish over the wall of the garden of nearby Burlington House. A more official version for the request was 'for the gratification of the publick and to give employment to industrious females'. In the original rules and regulations it is stated that, among other anti-social activities that were forbidden, were 'hurrying to the point of running', and perambulators. The latter, it was thought, would attract young soldiers to the nursemaids. Whistling was frowned upon as was the carrying of umbrellas, open or shut.

Retired soldiers act as 'arcade beadles' to maintain the necessary discipline and decorum. The Piccadilly entrance was rebuilt in 1911 to the designs of Beresford Pite.

44 – DEVONSHIRE HOUSE GATES, PICCADILLY

Augustus Hare, in his *Walks in London*, 1901, volume two, refers to Devonshire House as being as a 'perfectly unpretending building'. It replaced Berkeley House, built for Sir John Berkeley and destroyed by fire in 1733. Originally, the gates were made for Lord Cavendish's house at Turnham Green, and when the house was demolished in 1838 they were moved to his house at Chiswick, only to be moved once more, this time to the Devonshire House in Piccadilly.

They survived here until 1924, when a large office building was erected on the site. The then Office of Works, now known as English Heritage, bought the gates and erected them in the railing of the Piccadilly side of Green Park. In their present position they lead nowhere, and make no pretence of being in any way useful. The family coat-of-arms remains on the top of the gates.

45 – GAS LIGHTS AT BUCKINGHAM PALACE

Part of the re-development of the area from Buckingham Palace to Trafalgar Square was the re-siting of The Mall between 1904 and 1911. This entailed putting up new railings and gates in front of the palace; the gateway's piers were lit by gas lanterns supported by large stone fish. In spite of the advance of street lighting, these lamps are still run on gas. One result of re-aligning The Mall was the removal of a milk fair (a City dairy) from the palace end. Here cows were housed in sheds and fresh milk dispersed.

46 – STATUE OF QUEEN VICTORIA, QUEEN'S GARDENS

Standing at the palace end of The Mall is an elaborate statue of Queen Victoria, the work of Sir Thomas Brock. It is made from white marble, stands 82ft high, weighs 2,300 tons and is crowned by a gilt Victory. The figure of the Queen is 13ft high. The observant will see that the queen has a new nose. The story is that careless workmen were removing the scaffolding at the end of a cleaning operation and one scaffold pole fell!

47 – Galleon-topped lamp-posts, The Mall

These galleon-topped lamp-posts line the way from Admiralty Arch to Buckingham Palace. They form part of the National Memorial to Queen Victoria of 1903-1904, when The Mall's character was radically altered. The work was completed in 1911 when the new route was officially opened after it had been widened to its present width.

Admiralty Arch was designed by Sir Aston Webb and comprises three deep arches, each with wrought iron gates. The two side arches are used by traffic entering or leaving The Mall from Trafalgar Square.

48 – GIRO'S HEADSTONE, CARLTON HOUSE TERRACE

This marks the grave of Giro, a dog owned by Leopold von Hoesch, the German Ambassador in the early 1930s. It is beside a building that was first occupied by the Prussian legation, and that became the German Embassy after the unification of Germany in 1871. When Giro died in February, 1934, the Ambassador asked permission to bury him in the small garden beside the embassy. The inscription on the stone reads:

'GIRO'
EIN TREUER BEGLEITER!
LONDON IM FEBRUAR 1934
HOESCH

49 – CABINET WAR ROOMS, KING CHARLES STREET

At the end of King Charles Street, from Whitehall, steps lead down to Winston Churchill's Cabinet War Rooms. During the dark days of the Second World War, Churchill and his Chiefs of Staff masterminded Britain's war efforts from this complex of underground rooms beneath Whitehall.

50 – QUEEN ANNE HOUSES, QUEEN ANNE'S GATE

Here is one of the 'lost' eighteenth century corners of London, named after the reigning monarch of the time – Queen Anne. Until the late nineteenth century Queen Anne's Gate was two separate closes divided by a wall that stretched across the roadway to where the statue of Queen Anne now stands. To the east was Park Street, and the west Queen Square. After the wall came down they became Queen Anne's Gate.

The over-mantels of the doorways are of wood painted white to simulate the Coade stone figures above the windows. This artificial stone was manufactured by the Coade family on the South Bank where the Royal Festival Hall now stands. The figures, of grotesques, kings and queens, were carved, in reverse, in a solid block of wood; the liquid substance of the faux stone was poured in and allowed to set hard before being turned out. The formula for the stone was lost when the last member of the family died childless.

51 – STATUE OF QUEEN ANNE, QUEEN ANNE'S GATE

There is a 'moving' story to this statue (sculptor unknown), whose presence has been recorded in several places in and around Westminster. An old print of the parish church of St Mary le Strand shows it over the portico, while another authority records that it was intended to be placed at the top of a 150ft column in the Strand. Gleichen, in *London Open-air Statuary*, writes: 'It is believed to have been erected (here) in the early eighteenth century through the loyalty of William Paterson founder of the Bank of England.' Believing the statue to be 'Bloody Mary' local children used to throw stones at it, calling on the Queen to chase them. However, Queen Anne is said to leave her pedestal on the anniversary of her death on August 1.

52 – Campanile of Westminster Cathedral

Rising 284ft into the sky, the campanile houses the cathedral's bells (cast in 1910) – one of which is the 'Edward Bell', dedicated to St Edward the Confessor, the founder of the present Westminster Abbey. It bears an inscription that reads:

> *While the sound of this bell travels through the clouds*
> *may the band of angels pray for those assembled in the*
> *church. Saint Edward pray for England.*

The cathedral's lift takes passengers to viewing points towards the top of the tower. From here, on a fine day, there are views from the hills of North London to the Downs in the south – as well as a good

peep into the grounds of Buckingham Palace.

The tower is surmounted by an 11ft cross that contains a relic of the True Cross.

53 – West doorway, Westminster Cathedral

After the restoration of the hierarchy of the Roman Catholic Church in 1850 a site off Victoria Street was found to establish a cathedral for the Archbishop of Westminster. John Francis Bentley was commissioned to design it. The structure of the building was finished and consecrated in 1910, although to this day much of the interior remains unfinished. The entrance is through one of the west doorways. The Latin inscription above the doorway translates as:

Lord Jesus, King and Redeemer save us by your Blood

This is an early reference to the dedication of the cathedral to The Precious Blood of Our Lord and Saviour Jesus Christ. In the tympanum is a mosaic by Robert Bell that depicts Jesus Christ holding a book with the words, in Latin, that are best translated as: *I am the gate, if any one enters by Me he will be saved.* On either side are figures of Our Lady with St Joseph, St Peter with the Keys of Heaven and St Edward the Confessor with his ring. Medallions of stone on either side of the doorway show twelve early Archbishops of Canterbury from St Augustine, 597, to St Boniface, 1254.

54 – Little Ben, Victoria Street

For seventy-five years Little Ben was the meeting place for French people before they caught the Dover train at Victoria Station to return home. It was removed, temporarily, for road-widening but did not return for some seventeen years. Meanwhile the clock spent some time in the workshops of John Smith and Sons of Derby, where it was completely restored and given a new mechanism. Elf

Aquitaine, the French oil company financed the restoration and the return of the clock to its original home at the Victoria end of Vauxhall Bridge.

It stands 30ft high and is a miniature version of St Stephen's Clock Tower (Big Ben) at the other end of Victoria Street. The inscription on the side of the clock reads:

'Little Ben'
First erected in 1892. Taken down 1964.
Restored and re-erected on the 15th December 1981
By Westminster City Council
With the help of ELF Aquitaine UK
Offered as a gesture of Franco-British Friendship.
Little Ben's apology for Summer Time
My hands you may retard or may advance
My heart beats true for England as for France
JWR
Restored and rebuilt 1981 by
John Smith & Sons
Midland Clock Works Ltd
Derby

55 – Clock face, Parliament Square

On the north clock face of St Stephen's Clock Tower (which houses the world famous Big Ben bell), there is an interesting inscription in Latin. It reads:

Domine Salvan Fag Nostram Victoriam Primam

This translates as 'Oh Lord save our Queen Victoria the First'. Although it is customary to 'number' kings and queens of the same name, usually the practice commences only after the first.

56 – Middlesex Guildhall, Parliament Square

The Guildhall, once the administrative headquarters of the county of Middlesex, was built between 1906 and 1913 to the designs of JS Gibson and Partners. Today it is used as a Crown Court. It stands on the site of the detached bell tower of Westminster Abbey. The stone carvings above the doorway – the work of Henry C Fehr – depict historical scenes including the signing of Magna Carta at Runnymede near Windsor in 1215, and the offering of the Crown to Lady Jane Grey, 'the nine days queen', in 1553. Lady Jane had been nominated by Henry VIII to succeed Edward VI to prevent the Catholic Mary from becoming queen. But the popular choice was Mary and Lady Jane was beheaded.

57 – KING STREET BOUNDARY MARKER, PARLIAMENT SQUARE

All that is left of a once noble street is a plaque on the balustrade of a government office on the north side of Parliament Square.

Vanished King Street began as a means for riders to by-pass the mansion and grounds of the De Burgh family that occupied the land between Bridge Street and Charing Cross. It had acquired its name by the fifteenth century when it had become a desirable residential street, being so close to the royal palace of St Stephen at Westminster. In the seventeenth century Oliver Cromwell bought a house there and entertained his chiefs of staff there 'at his house in King Street'.

Between 1683 and 1686 a building development on the west side became Downing Street, named after Sir George Downing, a diplomat who served both Oliver Cromwell and Charles II with equal devotion . A survey of 1720, reported in Strype's eighteenth century revised edition of John Stow's *Survay of the Cities of London and Westminster,* first published in 1598, records:

> *Downing Street, a pretty open Place, especially at the upper end, where are four or five very large and well-built Houses, fit for persons of Honour and Quality; each House having a pleasant Prospect into St James's Park, with a Tarras Walk.*

The street survived various alterations and additions until 1899, when the existing buildings were demolished and replaced by new public offices, and the street merged with Parliament Street.

58 – ROMAN BOUNDARY STONE, WESTMINSTER ABBEY

Lying buried in the ground of the former churchyard of St Margaret's is a stone considered by some to mark a tomb – but actually it is a boundary stone from Roman times. The jurisdiction of the Roman Governor of the City of London (Londinium) was marked around its outskirts by such stones. Presumably this was the second (it is marked II) of a number of other stones, all of which have now disappeared. The church and abbey stand on the former Thorney Island at the estuary of the River Tyburn, close to where the legendary temple dedicated to Apollo stood until its destruction in an earthquake.

<u>59</u> – Crimean War memorial, Westminster Abbey

In front of Westminster Abbey stands a red granite column surmounted by a statue of St George and the dragon. Designed by George Gilbert Scott, it commemorates old boys of Westminster School killed in the Crimean War and the Indian Mutiny.

As well as St George, there are statues of Edward the Confessor, Henry III (both were builders of Westminster Abbey), Elizabeth I (second founder of the school) and Queen Victoria, in whose reign the war and mutiny occurred.

There are four stone lions at the foot of the column. Sculptor J Birnie Philip was responsible for all the figures except St George, which was the work of JR Clayton.

60 – STREET SIGN, COWLEY STREET

Street signs first appeared in the seventeenth century at a time when literacy was increasing and the use of picture signs decreasing. Few of the tablets remain *in situ*, but this is one of them. Street tablets were decorative devices or inscriptions in stone that, usually, gave little more than a name. Many are now in the care of the Museum of London, on London Wall. The oldest and most interesting is one showing a man holding a gardening spade, and the date 1670. It stood at the end of Gardener's Lane, which has long since disappeared.

61 – PUBLIC SHELTER NOTICE, LORD NORTH STREET

At the outbreak of the Second World War in 1939 a number of coal storage vaults under the pavements of the capital were strengthened and offered as public air raid shelters. Lord North Street still has three examples of the notices on the house walls showing passers-by the way to a shelter.

Today many of the houses in the street are lived in by Members of Parliament as the locality is 'within the call of the Division Bell'. Bells are installed in their homes to call them back to the House to vote.

62 – PINEAPPLE, LAMBETH BRIDGE

Pineapples on top of slender stone obelisks at either end of Lambeth Bridge are a reminder of the work of the seventeenth century horticulturalist, John Tradescant, who first brought these and other exotic fruits and plants to England. Today the name and work of the family is continued and commemorated in the Tradescant Museum housed in the former parish church of Lambeth, St Mary's, at the southern end of the bridge. Within the churchyard are the tomb of the Tradescants – and of Admiral (Captain) Bligh. Part of the churchyard has been transformed into a seventeenth century garden which contains only plants grown by the Tradescants.

The present bridge, the second, was opened in 1932 by George V.

63 – Buxton drinking fountain, Victoria Tower Gardens

This ornate fountain commemorates the emancipation of slavery in the former British Empire. Originally put up in the north west corner of Parliament Square in 1865, it was moved here in 1951 when traffic in the square was re-organised. The fountain is named after the nineteenth century social reformer, Sir Thomas Fowell Buxton MP, who fought for the abolition of slavery and prison reform. It was designed by his son, Charles, and paid for by public subscription. The fountain is octagonal in shape and of polished pink granite, grey stone and white marble. On the corners are bronze statuettes of British rulers from Caratacus (41-51AD) to Queen Victoria.

64 – CENOTAPH, WHITEHALL

Once described as 'a triumph of exquisite simplicity', the Cenotaph is also a marvellous optical illusion with not one straight line in the whole structure. It is a perfect example of entasis (whereby actual convexity corrects the illusion of concavity). All its lines describe gentle arcs so that its perpendiculars and horizontals meet at points 900ft away.

Sir Edwin Lutyens designed it for the 1919 Peace Procession, and it

was constructed originally of plasterboard. The structure was so fragile that London Fire Brigade was called in to place a wreath on the top.

The design caught the imagination of the public and a stone version was erected a year later. Here, every November, the monarch leads a national service of remembrance for the fallen of two world wars. The word cenotaph means, literally, empty tomb.

65 – WEATHERVANE ON THE BANQUETING HOUSE

The Banqueting House was designed by Inigo Jones as part of a vast 'new' Whitehall Palace that was to replace one that had been burnt to the ground. It was the first purely Renaissance building in London when it was completed in 1622. However, the money ran out before the remainder of the palace complex was built.

The weathervane on its roof was one of those put up by James II on all the royal palaces so that he could know immediately when a south-westerly wind was blowing. A wind from this quarter could signal that William of Orange (William III) was about to set sail for England and, with his wife Mary II (James's sister), claim the throne. After his worst fear was realised, James made several abortive attempts to regain the throne. He died in 1699, aged sixty-six, at St Germaine in France.

The house, which may be visited for a fee, is looked after by English Heritage.

66 – BUST OF CHARLES I, WHITEHALL

In a niche above the entrance to the Banqueting House is an eighteenth century bust of Charles I; the sculptor has been listed as 'unknown' but some experts claim it to be by Bernini. It was placed here in 1950 by Hedley Hope-Nicholson, the secretary of the Society of King Charles the Martyr – it being one of three busts of Charles that he had found, quite by chance, in a builder's yard in Fulham.

It was from an opening in the wall above the bust that Charles I stepped on January 30, 1649, to his public beheading on the scaffold in front of the building. Afterwards the head was sewn back on to the body and the corpse was laid in a coffin in the Great Hall. A loyalist visitor paying his last respects to his king noticed one of the curtains at the windows move. A shadowy figure, identified as Oliver Cromwell, left the room, allegedly muttering 'It need never to have happened'. The body was taken to Windsor Castle where Charles was laid to rest in the crypt of St George's Chapel.

Of the two other busts found at Fulham, one may be seen in a niche on the outside of St Margaret's Church, Westminster, where the king looks across at his adversary, Oliver Cromwell; the other is in private hands.

67 - RIVERSIDE STEPS, VICTORIA EMBANKMENT

Between the Victoria Embankment and the Ministry of Defence are the riverside steps of the former Whitehall Palace. A plaque describes the stairs as being 'Queen Mary's Steps Whitehall', and dates them from 1691 when Sir Christopher Wren designed a waterside terrace for Mary II. The steps were uncovered during excavations for a new government office building in 1939. They have been left in the original position and show how much wider the Thames was in the seventeenth century.

68 – HIGH TIDE HOUSE, WESTMINSTER BRIDGE

This metal open column building is marked on the inside in the form of a measure that enables the height of tides at Westminster Bridge to be registered.

69 – York House water gate, Embankment Gardens

Within sight of the Embankment underground station stands a sturdy reminder of the past – York House's water gate. Today the gate is fronted by the gardens that were created when the Victoria Embankment was built between 1864 and 1870 by Sir Joseph Bazalgette, at a cost of £1,260,000.

The river gate is the sole survivor of York House, once the home of Archbishops of York, and later given by James I to the first Duke of Buckingham. It is said that the second duke sold the house and grounds for building purposes but stipulated that any streets that were built on the site should bear his names and title. His names are still remembered in some of the streets behind the gate today, such as George Court, Villiers Street and Buckingham Street.

Inigo Jones designed the gate in the early seventeenth century and Nicholas Stone was responsible for the carvings. Over the central archway stands the coat of arms of the Duke of Buckingham, whose family motto was *Fidei coticula crux* (The touchstone of faith is the cross). The two lions on the top hold shields with anchors that symbolise the duke's service as Lord High Admiral.

70 – St Paul's church portico, Covent Garden

The church, consecrated in 1639, was designed by Inigo Jones for the Duke of Bedford. It was the first new Anglican church in London since the Reformation of the sixteenth century. Today, in addition to being a parish church, it is also the church for the Actors Church Union. The portico, which looks across to the former Covent Garden Market buildings, has one large and two smaller doorways, none of which lead anywhere, having been blocked in the nineteenth century when the interior of the building was re-oriented so that the altar is now against the east wall. The portico was the setting for George Bernard Shaw's *Pygmalion*, and the musical version, *My Fair Lady*. Today it is often used as a backdrop for the street performers of Covent Garden.

71 – FIRST PUPPET SHOW PLAQUE, COVENT GARDEN

Diarist Samuel Pepys records on May 9, 1662:
> '. . . thence to see an Italian puppet play, that is within
> the rails there – the best that ever I saw, and great resort of
> gallants . . .'

and on May 23, 1662:
> '. . . my wife and I to the puppet play in Covent Garden, which
> I saw the other day, and indeed it is very pleasant.'

The show is popularly supposed to be a survival of the old miracle plays, the character of Pontius Pilate having degenerated into that of Punch, while Judas Iscariot has, in the course of time, become a woman, Judy'.

NEAR THIS SPOT

PUNCH'S PUPPET SHOW

WAS

FIRST PERFORMED IN ENGLAND

AND WITNESSED BY

SAMUEL PEPYS

1662

This notice was caused to be inscribed by
The Society for Theatre Research and the
British Puppet and Model Theatre Guild
1962

72 – GOODWINS COURT, ST MARTIN'S LANE

At first glance through the archway that leads from St Martin's Lane, Goodwins Court seems to be a short *cul-de-sac*. Yet here can be found a perfect row of bow-fronted, late eighteenth century shops with living quarters above. This is a little piece of Regency London that is so easily missed by the passers-by in St Martin's Lane. The name is first mentioned in 1690 in the *Westminster Rate Book* of that year.

73 – Inscription, Church of St Martin in the Fields

D. Sacran aedem S. Martini Parachianai extrui A. A.
MDCCXXV1 Iacobo Gibbs Architecto

This translates as: 'The parishioners of St Martin's caused this building, dedicated to God, to be erected, AD 1726, James Gibbs architect'. The inscription on this Trafalgar Square church is an early example of a 'signed building' giving the name and profession of the designer.

James Gibbs was born in 1682, the younger son of Peter Gibbs of Footdeesmire, near Aberdeen 'a gentleman of an ancient family, and a small fortune'. His family were Roman Catholics and merchants who, by law, were prohibited from inheriting property, or educating their children. Gibbs was sent to an aunt in Holland for further education. His travels led him through France and Germany to Italy, where he was taught architecture by Carlo Fontana, surveyor to Pope Clement VI.

In 1709 he returned to Scotland, but there was little chance of his being offered work there, and he left for London. When the Fifty New Churches Building Act was passed in 1711 he was appointed surveyor to the scheme. His first London church was St Mary-Le-Strand in 1714, followed by St Martin's, built 1722-1726. Other Gibbs buildings in London include St Peter's Church in Vere Street (on which St Martin's was based) and Burlington House, Piccadilly.

74 – ROYAL COAT OF ARMS, ST MARTIN IN THE FIELDS

On the death of Queen Anne in 1714, the throne passed to the House of Hanover and the alteration of the Royal Coat of Arms once again. The new Arms consisted of first quarter England and Scotland, paled, second, France (until 1801), third, Ireland, and fourth, the Arms of the House of Hanover.

St Martin's is the parish church for Buckingham Palace, Clarence House and St James's Palace, and its registers record births, marriages and deaths in all three residences.

75 – BELFRY AND SPIRE, ST MARTIN IN THE FIELDS

Halfpence and farthings, say the bells of St Martin's, goes the line in the old nursery rhyme *Oranges and Lemons.* While there were six churches in the City of London dedicated to St Martin of Tours, it is always to the one in Trafalgar Square that the verse is attributed.

In the eighteenth century all the bells were recast by Abraham Rudhall of Gloucestershire. In 1987 St Martin's bells were sent to the Music Department of the University of Western Australia in Perth. In return the university provided the parish with 20 tons of copper and tin from Australian mines to have a lighter peal cast. The thirteen new bells, cast in the Whitechapel bell foundry, were installed in 1988.

The steeple, rebuilt in 1842, consists of a bell-stage with round-headed windows and coupled pilasters at the angles and, above, a recessed octagonal open lantern with attached colonettes. On top is a pierced concave-sided spire.

76 – STATUE OF JAMES II, NATIONAL GALLERY

Tobias Rustick, the Keeper of Hampton Court and Yeoman of the Robes to Charles II, commissioned and paid for this Grinling Gibbons statue, and had it placed in the privy gardens behind the Banqueting House in Whitehall, on New Year's Day, 1687. It cost £300 and shows the king in Roman dress.

Rustik also commissioned Gibbons to produce a companion statue,

of James II's elder brother, Charles II. This may be seen in the Centre Court of the Royal Chelsea Hospital.

The James II statue was moved in August 1897 to the garden of Gwydyr House (facing Whitehall). At the time of the Coronation of Edward VII in 1902 it was removed in order that a viewing stand could be erected in its place. For months afterwards it lay on its back among the grass and weeds of the garden, and it was not until December 1903 that it was removed to its present position outside the National Gallery in Trafalgar Square.

77 – PORTICO, NATIONAL GALLERY

Designed by William Wilkins, the gallery took six years to complete between 1832 and 1838. It was built to house the art collection of John Julius Angerstein, a Russian merchant and philanthropist. The gallery is known familiarly to many Londoners as the 'national cruet set' after the three domes that adorn its roof.

The portico came from Carlton House, Pall Mall, where the Prince Regent, later George IV, lived until the death of his father. Then, the house was demolished and Carlton House Terrace replaced it. Several of the fireplaces and doors were removed to Buckingham Palace and Windsor Castle.

On the site of the National Gallery England's kings once kept their hunting birds. The noise from these birds, particularly in the mating season, gave rise to the stables here being called 'mews', from their mewing.

78 – 'Bomb scars' on Nelson's Column

The damage at the foot of the western side of the monument has often been attributed to enemy action during either or both of the two world wars of the twentieth century. It was, however, the result of over-jubilant members of the armed forces celebrating in Trafalgar Square in 1918. Accidentally, they set fire to a workman's hut on the site. The flames and the heat were so fierce that the granite stone cracked and split.

79 – WPC Yvonne Fletcher's memorial, St James's Square

This is one of a number of memorials scattered throughout London that commemorate the bravery in the line of duty of the men and women of the Metropolitan Police Force. WPC Yvonne Fletcher was on crowd duty on April 17, 1984, outside the Libyan Embassy in the square, when she was shot. The Embassy was under siege at the time as a number of alleged terrorists were said to be sheltering inside the building.

80 – Eros, Piccadilly Circus

Known throughout the world as Eros, the figure on the top of the memorial drinking fountain in Piccadilly Circus is not, in fact, the god of love, but the Christian Angel of Charity.

The fountain was built in memory of the seventh Earl of Shaftesbury and is a rebus on the earl's title. The figure with the archer's bow has released an arrow (shaft) that has buried itself in some distant plot of ground – shaft+bury. Water still trickles down the memorial. The drinking cups originally provided have long since been taken by souvenir hunters.

PUBLIC TRANSPORT

Listed here are the nearest underground stations to the start (S) and the finish (F) of the walks.

MF – Monday to Friday. MS – Monday to Saturday. SU – Sunday only.
Buses with disabled access – 3, 17, 25, 55, 56, 77A, 88, 115, 139

Route one   (S) Temple Station (closed Sunday) – Circle and
                   District Lines.
                   Buses – nearest from Strand, 4 (MF), 6, 9, 11, 13, 15, 23
                   (MS), 77A, 91, 172, 176.
                   (F) Monument Station – Circle, District and Northern
                   Lines.
                   Buses – 15

Route two   (S) Tower Hill – Circle and District Lines
                   Buses – 15, 25 (MF)
                   (F) Tower Hill – Circle and District Lines
                   Buses – 15, 25 (MF)

Route three   (S) Aldgate Circle and Metropolitan Lines
                   Buses – 15, 25 (MF), 40, 42, 67, 78, 100, 115, 253
                   (F) Mansion House – Circle and District Lines
                   Buses – 15, 17, 25 (MF), 521 (MF)

Route four   (S) St Paul's – Central Line
                   Buses – 8, 22B, 25, 56, 501 (MF), 521 (MF)
                   (F) St Paul's – Central Line
                   Buses – 8, 22B, 25, 56, 501 (MF), 521 (MF)

Route five   (S) St Paul's – Central Line
                   Buses – 8, 22B, 25, 56, 501 (MF), 521 (MF)
                   (F) St Paul's – Central Line
                   Buses – 8, 22B, 25, 56, 501 (MF), 521 (MF)

Route six   (S) Moorgate – Circle, City and Hammersmith, and
                   Metropolitan Lines
                   Buses – 4 (MF), 21 (MF), 133, 141 (SU)
                   (F) St Paul's – Central Line
                   Buses – 8, 22B, 56, 501 (MF), 521 (MF)

Route seven   (S) Hyde Park Corner – Piccadilly Line
Buses – 2, 8, 16, 36, 38, 52, 73, 82, 185 (from Victoria)
Buses – 8, 9, 14, 19, 22, 38 (from Piccadilly and
Knightsbridge)
(F) Green Park – Jubilee, Piccadilly and Victoria Lines
Buses – 8, 9, 14, 19, 22, 38

Route eight   (S) St James's Park – Circle and District Lines
Buses – 11, 24, 211, 507 (MF) (alight at Broadway stop
in Victoria street)
(F) Victoria – Circle, District and Victoria Lines
Buses – 11, 24, 211, 507 (MF)

Route nine   (S) Westminster – Circle, Jubilee and District Lines
Buses – 3, 11, 12, 24, 53, 77A, 88, 159 (Whitehall stop)
(F) Pimlico – Victoria Line
Buses – 24 (Belgrave Road), C10 (Lupus Street)
2, 36,185 (Vauxhall Bridge Road)

Route ten   (S) Westminster – Circle, District and Jubilee Lines
Buses – 3, 11, 12, 24, 53, 77A, 88, 159 (Whitehall stop)
(F) Westminster – Circle, District and Jubilee Lines
Buses – 3, 11, 12, 24, 53, 77A, 88, 159 (Whitehall stop)

Route eleven   (S) Charing Cross - Bakerloo and Northern Lines
Buses – 6, 9, 11, 13, 15, 23, 77A, 91, 176
(F) Piccadilly Circus - Bakerloo and Piccadilly Lines
Buses – 3, 6, 7, 8, 10, 12, 13, 15, 23, 25 (MF), 53, 55, 73,
88, 139, 176

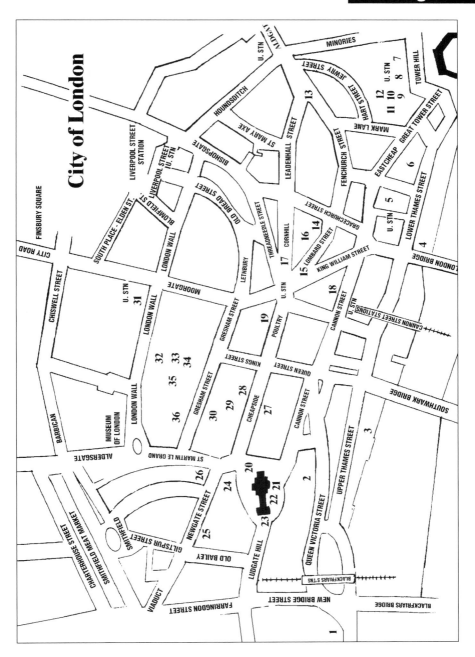

City of London

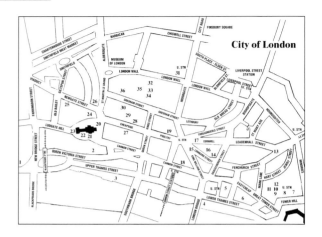

01	Victoria Embankment	19	Poultry
02	Queen Victoria Street	20	St. Paul's Cathedral
03	Queenhithe	21	Cloisters' foundations
04	London Bridge	22	St. Thomas Becket
05	Pudding Lane	23	Statute of Queen Anne
06	St. Dunstan's Hill	24	Paternoster Steps
07	Trinity Square	25	Warwick Lane
08	Tower Hill	26	Newgate Street
09	Muscovy Street	27	Cheapside
10	Seething Lane	28	Honey Lane
11	Hart Street	29	Wood Street
12	St. Olave's, Hart Street	30	Gresham Street
13	Leadenhall Street	31	London wall
14	Lombard Street	32	Silver Street/Noble Street
15	Hanging Street signs	33	Aldermanbury
16	Exchange Alley	34	Heminge & Condell
17	Cornhill	35	Wood Street
18	Cannon Street	36	Noble Street

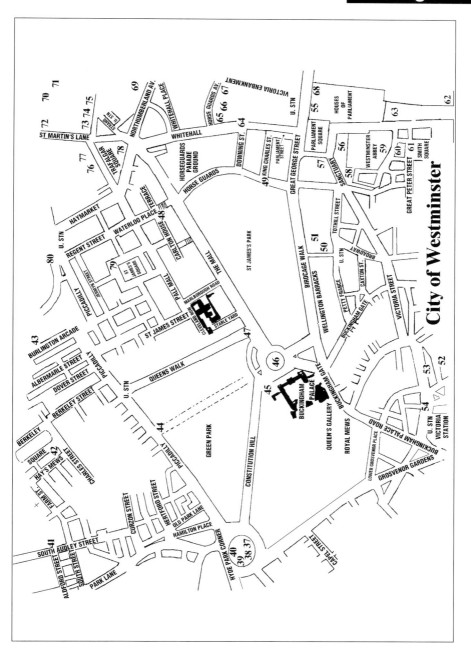

City of Westminster

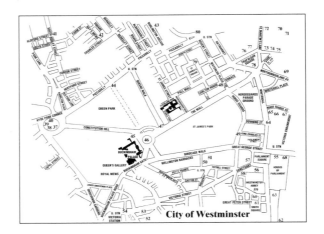

City of Westminster

37	Wellington Arch	60	Cowley Street sign
38	Royal Artillery memorial	61	Lord North Street
39	Mary with the Christ Child	62	Lambeth Bridge - pineapple
40	Mess tin, SRD	63	Buxton Drinking fountain
41	Grosvenor Chapel	64	Whitehall - Cenotaph
42	Running footman	65	Banqueting House weathervane
43	Burlington Arcade		
44	Devonshire House gates	66	Whitehall - bust of Charles I
45	Buckingham Palace gas lights	67	Whitehall Palace river steps
46	Queen Victoria's statue	68	Westminster Bridge high tide
47	The Mall - lampost	69	York House
48	"Giro's" grave	70	St. Paul's church, Covent Garden
49	Cabinet War rooms		
50	Queen Anne's Gate	71	First puppet show plaque
51	Queen Anne's statue	72	Goodwins Court
52	Westminster Cathedral	73	Iacobo Gibbs Architecto
53	West doorway	74	George I Royal Coat of Arms
54	"Little Ben"	75	St. Martin in the Fields
55	"Big Ben's" Clock face	76	James II - National Gallery
56	Middlesex Guildhall	77	National Gallery - portico
57	Site of King Street	78	Nelson's Column
58	Roman boundary stone	79	St. James's Square
59	Crimean War memorial	80	"Eros"

ABOUT THE AUTHOR

Charles Bird is a retired lecturer in the field of adult education. In 1949, after leaving the armed forces – where he was an education instructor – he returned to his own studies and subsequently graduated in European history.

His particular interests are the history of the English theatre, and the history of London, and as well as writing about London, he has built up a firm reputation in the capital as a compiler of graces to be said or sung before livery luncheons and dinners.

Titles soon to be added to his list of publications include:

A Guide to Literary London
Shrines of Yesterday and Today
What's That?
Sites of London
Americans in London
London's Mews, Parks and Squares
A Postcode Guide to Haunted London
Wesley's London

S. B. Publications publish a wide range of guides, local history and walking books. For a list of available titles, write for a free catalogue to:

S. B. Publications
19 Grove Road, Seaford, East Sussex BN25 1TP

Telephone: 01323 893498
E-mail: sbpublications@tiscali.co.uk
www: sbpublications.co.uk

Notes

Notes